ELIZABETH JENNINGS

Times and Seasons

CARCANET

For Simon Hornby

Some of these poems have appeared in the *Tablet*, *PN Review*, the *Spectator* and other journals, to whose editors thanks are due.

First published in 1992 by
Carcanet Press Limited
208-212 Corn Exchange
Manchester M4 3BQ

A CIP catalogue record for this book is
available from the British Library.
ISBN 0 85635 977 7

The publisher acknowledges financial assistance
from the Arts Council of Great Britain

100996758

Set in 10pt Palatino by Bryan Williamson, Darwen
Printed and bound in England by SRP Ltd, Exeter

821 JENN 05

Contents

Grammar

Allow, admit the brave, attentive verb,
Be patient, watch it, keep a distance off,
Think of an adjective, do not disturb

The music as it comes but let it move
Around, among the words. Now you must curb
Intruding conjugations, hold them off.

Listen, permit a polished noun. No rough
Rhythm must ride or intervene or rub
And rinse away. Here is the leash of love,

The love of speech and the perfection of
A tongue that's true, an ear that is an orb
Round which the very stars have room enough

For music of the spheres which will absorb
The awkward sentences and make them live
Where prepositions dance and adverbs lob

Their meaning wide but leashed by 'but' or 'if'.

Parts of Speech

I *Verb*

Listen, the acute verb
Is linking subject and object –
Hear the links fall in place
And the sturdy padlock clinking.

A verb is a power in all speech,
Rings through prose and verse.
It brings to birth. Can't you hear
The first cry of awareness?

'I go', 'I forget', 'I exist'
By language only and always.
Blood cannot beat in a void
And the potent, fiery tongue

Offers the gift of language,
Blesses our lips and throats.
'I love you' vows and connects
And moves in a climate of tensions.

II *Adjective*

I'm a close relative
    Of nouns, I reinforce
Their moods and meanings, I live
    By running on a course

They also move on. I
    Live by music too,
The run and scheme and cry
    That rises to the blue

Taut skies. I qualify
    And temper every noun,
Enrich it, help it fly.
    I'm never on my own.

Say 'Love' and you must add
    'Sweet love', 'dear love' and make
Your message deeper, lead
    To love for its rich sake.

III *Noun*

I preen myself, I am a peacock word,
    I am a call, am one
Who does not need a tether or a cord,
    I dally in the sun

And in the life of grammar take a part
    That is a main one. You
Can never do without me. I'm the heart
    And teller of what's true.

IV *Adverb*

I qualify, I add to, I insist
   That verbs are active, go
About their business aptly. I exist
   Mainly to let them show

How graceful and how many-natured are
   Their meanings and their tense
Purposes. I show them how to wear
   Any experience

With a fine gesture. Yet I also can
   Help them to hide and go
Into small cells where they tell what a man
   Can shape alone. I show

Verbs they are needy on their busy own.
   I hand right clothes out and
Help them to speak a need or use a phone
   And how to understand.

For My Mother

I *My Mother Dying Aged 87*

You died as quietly as your spirit moved
All through my life. It was a shock to hear
Your shallow breathing and more hard to see
Your eyes closed fast. You did not wake for me
But even so I do not shed a tear.
Your spirit has flown free

Of that small shell of flesh. Grandchildren stood
Quietly by and it was they who gave
Most strength to us. They also loved you for
Your gentleness. You never made them fear
Anything. The memories you leave
Are happy times. You were

The one who gave me stamps and envelopes
And posted all my early poems. You had
Such faith in me. You could be firm and would
Curb tantrums, and would change an angry mood
With careful threats. I cannot feel too sad
Today for you were good

And that is what the kindly letters say.
Some are clumsy, some embarrass with
Lush piety but all will guide your ship
Upon a calm, bright ocean and we keep
Our eyes on it. It is too strong for death
And so we do not weep.

II *Grief*

I miss my mother today.
I went into a shop and saw the Mothering Sunday
    Cards in bright array.
I always used to send her one and now
    There is nothing to write or say.

    Grief can strike you when
You least expect it. It's an emptiness
    Easy to fill with pain.
My mother had no rage, was always kind.
    When will she come again

And darken and haunt the large room of my mind?

III *Her Birthday*

My mother would be eighty-eight today.
It has been cool, no April fit for her
And yet, and yet, she always had a way
Of liking weather as it came. There were
No angry days for her,

No sky she did not watch and no downpour
That wasn't welcome in some way. I wish
I owned this quality. My mother's power
Lay in a gentle steadfastness. No rash
Judgments spread from her

And yet, although not witty, she would have
The perfect phrase for an unfit event.
When we were on a roundabout she gave
A straight look at 'hot gospellers' who went
By. 'Why should they move

'About like that with sandwich-boards which say
"Thy judgment is at hand" and spoil our fun
That's innocent enough?' I think today
Of words like that and wish her back upon
Her eighty-eighth birthday.

IV *A Memory*

Nothing is innocent,
Nothing unable to alter, to carry a word
  Of yours. Each element
Is charged with a copy of you or carries a chord
  Or echo of something you said.
Today in a blackbird's joyful cry I heard
  You speaking from the dead.

  The usual memories
At the front of my mind are wholly happy ones,
  Your aim was always to please,
Especially children. You possessed innocence
  Yourself, were a person of peace
And now you have no control over circumstance
  But are part of the ironies

  Of death and grief. One night
When I was a child I was crying loudly because
  I had seen a saint with a white
Veil on his face in a London cathedral. It was
  Simply guessing at the sight
Beneath that cover that scared me. My noisy tears
  Brought you. You switched on the light

  And somehow quickly found
What was the matter. You spoke the right words at once.
  I heard the redeeming sound
'He'll be laughing at you in Heaven.' Innocence
  Returned and I was bound
Again within the safety you'd built. No defence

  Is round me now. Those good
Words can start the flowing tears again
  And what once your words withstood
Is itself a cause for all the expert pain
  Your love healed once, and the mood
Of relief is altered, yet grief has become a gain
  Because it means gratitude.

V *Sudden Remembrance*

Orphaned and elderly and yet a child,
For so I am when thoughts of you return,
Return and batter me and I'm not mild
But close to tears and scarred for these tears burn.
You tamed me when most wild,

You comforted my nightmares, came and sat
Beside my bed when sleep was far away.
You were a healing presence. More than that,
You were a joy, a treasure, could display
High spirits when the flat

Dull mood took charge of me. You always were
Busy and quick and swift to suffer too,
But only now and then did I know fear
When I could see a troubled look on you.
Tonight you feel so dear.

It is a cold wet June, the flowers are blown
In tangled throngs, the charcoal clouds hang near
The tousled tree-tops. Had we ever known
So dull a June? I doubt it. How I care
For you. Where have you gone?

My faith speaks of another life and I
Find your nature a right proof of that.
A child, I'd have you crowned up in the sky,
And growing old I see your star well set.
O your death will not die.

VI *Her Wisdom*

The paper's badly crumpled. You a bride
Stare shyly, do not seem at ease with flowers
So strictly cut and, very close beside,
My father stands triumphant in full powers
Of thirty years. You hide

The look of fear, half-knowing what's to come
But only half because facts aren't enough.
Perhaps you thought of the new-polished home,
The wedding gifts. He looks at you with love,
Protectively. There's some

Hint of his patience. In his gazing eyes
His care of you is manifest. He would
Tell me years later he had to be wise
And wait for love's fulfilment for a good
Month and this defies

Our haste today and lack of thought. Also,
My mother, you were never much at ease
When I asked awkward questions. Later you –
Rightly now I think – told me it was
Fear of hurting. So

I learnt of sex and birth in furtive ways
With worried stares at magazines but now,
Thinking of childhood when you dressed my days
With paths and hedges, offering each bough
Of apples to me, I can only praise
Your care and wonder how

You stayed so gentle. I was stormy and
Quick to see a fault. You guided me
With love. In every poem I see your hand,
Your pride in those that did not need to be
Ones you could understand.

19

VII *More than an Elegy*

What are you now then?
   A thought on the wind?
A balance of spirit and air?
   A released mind?

You are more, more than this
   Though sometimes seem less,
You are the pain death is
   And yet you bless.

Let me not intervene,
   Mark my shadow where
Only you now have been,
   Your spirit is there

Where at best faith carries the heart.
   You are both air,
And earth and you are part
   Of a disciplined fire.

Let my missing you be
   What sometimes prayer
Is when it moves free.
   Let me find you there.

But the daily truth is
   That I see most
In physical memories,
   You are never a ghost.

How curious love can be
   For now your death
Shows me how lovingly
   The voice finds breath,

The hands find useful things
   To do. O you are
The way a blackbird sings
   And shapes the air.

VIII *Let Me Learn*

Let me learn from you now
  Or is it too late?
The North wind starts to sough,
  Coal shifts in the grate.

Once in a white and high
  Nursery we played as if
The ceiling were the sky,
  Each hour all life.

You and my father came
  After a dance
Bringing bright favours home.
  It still enchants

To think of you young as then.
  Your face never was
Wrinkled with lines even when
  Death took its place

Within you, beside you, all
  About. I was dry
With sorrow but tears do fall
  Now. You don't die

Over and over but are
  Installed beside
The pile of books laid here,
  The lamplight wide.

You read in bed, I feel
  Your heart stirring in mine
And everything starts to heal.
  What a delicate line

Death writes when love was the drift
  Of a life like yours.
At all my fears you laughed
  And cast out their force.

There will be no wind tonight,
   No angry words
And at dawn a strong light
   And chattering birds.

Poems, praise, prayer –
   In these I find
Your gentle atmosphere,
   Your steady mind.

IX *Her Gifts*

Most you return when fear is mastered. I
In childhood trembled often in the night,
Lay huddled and afraid to turn my face
Curtained by fingers. I had no near light.
How far the day-world was.

I could have called. I never did but vowed
Next morning I would ask for night-lights or
A bedside lamp. But then birds sang so loud,
The postman was so busy at the door
That all the dismal crowd

Of night's imagined terrors disappeared.
But then from six to ten I often ailed,
Fell against trees, picked up most germs. You heard
My hoarse cough and immediately you sailed
Without a sound or word

Into my room like a strong ship and gave
Me warm drinks, puffed the pillows and then sat
And read to me. I never had enough
Of your soft voice, firm hands. You sweetly taught
Me then the Tale of Love,

Its patience and forbearance and the way
It laughs off dread. How rich indeed I was
From your deep mine of gold. It shone each day.
Now you are dead but memories like these
Have taught me to obey

The kind impulse to give, the wish to share
My books, ideas I read, the jokes I'm told.
In laughter now I find you are most near
And, oddly maybe, you are never old
But the young mother who cast out my fear
And kept me from the cold.

X *My Debt*

I had a lucky childhood. I was
A late-developer and so I lived
For untimed weeks and months in any place
I could imagine. I think you perceived
This joyous state of grace,

For I was left to play alone although
You were below or in the garden and
Kept me safe as I ran quietly through
So many realms of gold. I would pretend
That I was priest, would go

Through all the stages of the Mass and be
Priest and server. On a string I held
A train. It was a thurible to me.
Sometimes in the garden I would build
Castles in air. You'd see

Within the child's busy mind, my world
Which you defended from a distance. Now
I know that you saw much more than you told.
Before the years of doubt and fear I'd go
About my worlds, a bold

Ruler sometimes, sometimes merely one
Who settled for a while. What better way
Can poets be prepared? I know of none.
I still am rich today

Since you would honour childhood's lack of time,
Its ignorance of clocks and bells and hours,
Its fascination with the world of rhyme,
You were the one who taught me my best powers –
Those fields of gold, those silver hills to climb,
Those gardens full of flowers.

The Smell of Chrysanthemums

The chestnut leaves are toasted. Conkers spill
Upon the pavements. Gold is vying with
Yellow, ochre, brown. There is a feel
Of dyings and departures. Smoky breath
    Rises and I know how Winter comes
    When I can smell the rich chrysanthemums.

It is so poignant and it makes me mourn
For what? The going year? The sun's eclipse?
All these and more. I see the dead leaves burn
And everywhere the Summer lies in heaps.
    I close my eyes and feel how Winter comes
    With acrid incense of chrysanthemums.

I shall not go to school again and yet
There's an old sadness that disturbs me most.
The nights come early; every bold sunset
Tells me that Autumn soon will be a ghost,
    But I know best how Winter always comes
    In the wide scent of strong chrysanthemums.

On the Tongue

The tang and touch on the tongue,
The pause, the creep, the quick advance and then
  The verbs which we move among,
The nouns that alter their meanings again and again,
  The poem which turns to song,

  The awkward adjective,
The thin-worn noun, the verb that seemed to grow stale.
  It is by language we live
For the senses falter, halt and finally fail,
  But in poems and only if

  We pay attention and stand
Listening, whispering, relishing a word,
  A rhyme, we discover the end
And purpose of art, the impulse which has heard
  A message it can lend

  And send us on with delight
And a soaring spirit which touches the furthest stars
  And makes a neighbour of night.
It draws refreshment out of dry discourse
  And animates dulled sight.

  A voice said 'Let there be song
When words join music in an intricate dance
  Which yet won't lead us wrong.
Let there be happiness as a sure defence
  Against shadows we move among

  And cannot wholly ignore'.
Yet I lift my pen and gaze at the heated day
  And am moved so intensely more
Than any human tongue can ever say,
  It is so quick and sure.

Protest after a Written Interview

They see you thus. You care and you are hurt
    At your self put on show.
How hidden its abasements, its wrung heart,
    How easily a blow

Opens the doors you thought were locked. They were
    Accessible to any
Who overruled a thought of care or fear
    Of ignominy.

So I am open and ridiculous!
    How pride can squirm at that.
My friend had saved me from all this, of course.
    I face the tit-for-tat

Of public criticism, fallings-short
    They understand too well.
I did not know my secret could be caught
    By any ready will,

And they are right. My work is not like me
    Though it's the world where I
Move, I believe, with right authority,
    But now I simply cry.

Yes, shed hot tears of childhood, waste my time
    By being laid so bare.
I'll get my poems in good dark shape and rhyme
    And always be armed there.

A Christmas Sequence

I *Advent*

Such movings, risings and such settings forth,
The world's astir with startings. Many go
From house to house seeking employment or
A room to live in. Voices everywhere
Are calling out loud slogans. War seems near
And there is easy fear.
Look at the mothers trying to seem calm,
See the sons and brothers who may be
Called up to go to war.

But this is also Advent, a good time
Once for a few and now for everyone.
A woman bears a child and carries it
Through the last month. She knows it is a son
And so does Joseph. Both are very poor
And their whole world is troubled. Romans have
Settled down and rule in Palestine.
Division, argument and pain are rife
But O a wonder's near,
A virgin girl is soon to give God life,
God as a man. How can we understand
That man can be divine?
We cannot but the centuries have told
This story as a fact and we believe.

O let us, even in our fear, join hands
As we think of a story that is old
Yet new each year. It is a mystery
How God took time and entered history.

What is she thinking now
   As they ride through the cold
Toward Bethlehem? O how
   Can her God who is old

Or outside time at least
   Be growing in her womb?
This girl does not look blessed
   She fills so little room

Yet carries a new truth,
   A God whom she makes man
Will soon take his first breath
   And fit a lofty plan.

How can we not feel love
   To see such helplessness?
Our cold hearts start to move
   With an old gentleness,

Yet it is new also
   Since we are feeling for
A God who is to grow
   To manhood like the poor.

Listen, let Mary sing
   Her unborn child a cry
Such as all mothers bring
   To their first lullaby.

His life was always one of contradiction:
A young girl, still a virgin gave him life,
He taught not happiness but dark affliction,
He spoke for peace when all around was strife.
He was a God whose action

Stirred the first stars, designed the universe,
Invented time, made men and gave them choice,
They disobeyed and he undid the curse
By being one of them. An infant's voice
Is sheltering each of us.

He chose our lot, was only different
In seeing evil but not being it.
It was with little things he was content
And made a world where even children fit
For he was innocent.

He died to rid mankind of bitterness
Since all that he would suffer was unjust,
And he showed love where love so seldom is –
In dark, in pain, in death. He took our dust
And taught it how to bless.

IV *The Shepherds*

He is so small the stars bow down
    The fierce winds ease their breath,
And careful shepherds look upon
    The one unsullied birth.
They kneel and stare while time seems gone
    And goodness rules the earth.

The blight on man is all undone
    And there will be no death,
For though this child will be nailed on
    A cross, he'll be so since
He is the jewel of untold worth,
    For him all stars have shone.

V *Hymn at the Crib*

Lord of failure, teach us your success
At sending up a glittering star again,
Lord of anguish, show us happiness,
Teach us your mysteries.

They open every locked door and they melt
The icy heart. Child of heaven and earth,
Teach us to eschew the smallest fault
And let us love all innocence. Your birth
Is where great kings have knelt

And where the poor of heart receive all gifts
The universe can offer. Christmas day
Lights all hearts, the humble man then lifts
The pride of centuries up. In Bread he may
Find all riches. Shafts

Of moonlight join the sun and every star
Bows to a child, the one of such great price,
Through him we learn that depths of sweetness are
Found where God makes his son a sacrifice,
And he is now and here

Binding the past and future till we stand
Only in a present. Paradise
Was once like this and when at last we mend
Our faults we shall again show gentle eyes
And generosity, and understand
That innocence is wise.

In Green Times

Let the blossom blow back to the tree,
Let the wind be lost in silences,
Let my childhood wake again round me,
    Its sweets and violences.

Out of that white nursery I came
Into the garden green to wade in deep.
Quiet broke with calling of my name.
    I acted half-asleep.

I listened to the bees. I felt the grass
Touch me softly. I would watch the sun
And every truant cloud that had to pass.
    I was at peace alone.

Nature was my shelter. All the berries
Plumped and showed their shining. I was there
In what could be a summer's dream. Time's worries
    Found no foot-hold near.

And nor did mine. Perspectives happened later.
All my world was flat and full of green.
Mountains face me. Rivers mirror me,
I am all aware and frightened too
But I can't turn back pages now to see
    What once was green and true.

A Child Destroyed

I can do nothing but feel, I can imagine
The terror within the mind of that child who was carried
Away from a moment of play. What did she see
In her mind's eye? Was it a happy regret?
Crumpets and milk? The children's TV programme?
He held the stinking cloth against her mouth
And she must have smelt tobacco, dirt, male stenches.
She tried to scream. She kicked him and he gripped
Her legs together, pinioned arms behind her.
Again and again I turn to my own childhood
When fears were but imaginary ones,
My only pains concussion or pneumonia,
And they seem honours as I try to force
Myself into this small child's little shoes
And clean white socks, and soft washed hair, and then
I bring her start in life to bear on me.
She knew of love in night-time kisses, hugs
And kind hands holding hers. Now this large weight,
The man's cruel body forcing her to lie
Under his. I hear her small frock torn.
I hope by then she was unconscious but
She may have felt the thrust and heave of sex,
Smelt the man's breath, and then he gripped her neck
And twisted it as if it were a bird's
Or else a rabbit's. So our world behaves.
We have grown lax and comfort-loving, watched
The act of sex on big screens in the dark,
Have eaten, drunk too much. We are to blame
And this small, broken, violated child
Must be the scapegoat. I'm ashamed and hate
The helplessness I feel, my world's cruel work.

Shapes and Surfaces

Edges of things, surfaces, smooth grain of wood,
Natural showing of rings of growth when a great
Tree is felled. Glass blown wide and light
Seen in Murano, seen in the Pueblo Espana
In Barcelona. All these things I praise –
Nature working with man or man with Nature.
I've walked on sea-shores when the tide was out
And picked up pebbles smoothed by hands of the sea,
Laid them on one another and observed the different
Shades of grey. What a bonus given by creation,
The working of time and tides on rock and crystal.
Then I've seen our Cotswold walls built patiently
With stones that are tapped and shaped, and thinned to lie
Upon each other in harmony, in order,
With only cement on top of the walls to hold
The flat stones lying side by side together.

Turner saw skies like this, he levelled or left
Entirely alone, responded to puff and billow,
Storm and calm, stress and peace. Again
Nature working with time, with space that is smoothed
Or ruffled or blown like glass, like a cherub's cheeks,
Never the same shapes twice. Never the same
Shade of pink or purple or gold or green
Seen exactly the same again. What a palette is here,
What a hoard of shapes and edges, surfaces, levels
And roughness Nature organises. No doubt
The sculptor learns from this when he gives pure form,
A Maillol or a Brancusi.
Creation is on the move out there in the sky,
In the land, in the sea, and here in my mind and of course
All in no time at all in the mind of God,
Smoother of stones, sculptor supreme and mason.
But he left so much for us to complete, to enjoy
And to use and to offer others. There is no end
To rounds and squares, angles and circles, no number
To colours and light. O there is the sun itself
Sculpting tomorrow as now the moon is shaping
Surfaces I shall never see. I ponder

Light years away, away in every sense
And light also in every meaning I know
And in shapes and spaces that never can be counted,
Now and tomorrow and always long ago.

A Litany for Contrition

Dew on snowdrop
        weep for me
Rain in a rose
        cleanse my heart,
Bud of crocus
        candle me to
Contrition. Far stars
        shine from your great
Heights, and burn my faults away.
Half-moon emerging
        from a cloud
Strengthen my spirit.
                All spring flowers,
More each day,
        in this night now
Give me a scent of our sweet powers.
A shower of rain
        wash me clean,
Let my spirit glow
        for I have seen
The terrible depth
        of dark in me.
Christ, you alone
        can cure jealousy.

My Ships

'When your ships come in' – the words in the nursery sounded
Every tidal pulse, all salty commands. I thought of
The shell I picked up one day and put to my ear
And indeed I heard the tide in another key
But not in one less true. The real sea's
Grace-notes were there, I remembered
The jetties the little sailing boats were roped to,
The smell of the rock-pools, my legs covered in seaweed,
My eyes searching for prawns. I pulled at limpets
But they resisted as all those ships resisted,
Were anchored somewhere I had not visited yet.
In my mind the blue sea brimmed, I knew the islands,
The cliffs and archipelagos. Ships sailed by
With sails taut for a moment straining with wind,

Tussling with gales, plucky against the white horses
Which reared and toppled. Some later ships were slowing,
Dawdled under the sun and little breezes,
The yachts slackened their sails, even the steamers
Seemed to drift. Here was a maritime childhood,
A world of minerals, salt pervasive, my ships
Shadows on nursery walls. I watched their prows
As I drifted off to a moonlit, tidal sleep,
Sailed in dreams not deeper than I had imagined
Only more foreign and excitable, only
More mysterious. I think the cargoes were words,
Hoards of adjectives, bales of nouns and sacks
Heavy with verbs. I woke to the shouting birds
Who sang all Summer under the nursery window.
All my world was broody with pollen and bird-song,
An inland burgeoning, gooseberries fattening, apples
Swelling and shining, but still the sea sang songs,
Hornpipe and heralding pipes, dog-watch and day-watch.

'When my ships come in' – prophetic words in a way
For what else is the roping and nailing of tea-chests but poems?
I know indeed the tug of the poem's tide,
Its being lifted and loosed at last on land
When the crane is drawn away and the sea subsides.

My ship is sailing still but sometimes it stands
On a motionless sea and it is motionless too,
As if at anchor. The sailors are sleeping, the storms
Blow and vex and heave in another quarter.
I try to sleep but a dream of sailing breaks through
My drowsiness. I cannot beckon my ships.
Their time is their own and no concern of mine
Or so it seems as I walk again through rock-pools
Savouring salt and iodine and brooding
In a world-wide dream of water.

Springtime and Easter

Love is leaping among the Spring's heavy branches,
Light torn from Winter clouds is forming new patterns,
Winning another year, another season
Of painful growing and delighted issue.
Light and music will come again after sunset,
Stricken clouds paling, darkening, disappearing,
Becoming the kindness of night-time, the later hours
Stretching out longer each evening,
Moving, dancing, pausing,
And the swallows returning, the hibernators waking,
The birth of the fledgeling, the cracking egg, the Easter candle,
So much occurring, so much enduring, so much renewal
And we are not ready, never are really prepared
For the love which whispered in Autumn, lay down in Winter
And is speaking now in a lark's voice shaping the sky
And singing the clouds away.

The love which hurt before it was spoken again
Dares to speak and we accept the pain
We know must arrive for if we surrender we always
Dare so much, risk a whole life almost
And some lack audacity.

We walked together under Spring-distressed branches
Thinking of words we did not speak, now and then
Touching finger on finger.
Then loosening the rosary of hands,
We let the light catch our mood, we heard a music
In skylark and swallow, in tumbling clouds and in rain,
Washing the world to beauty.
And we heard a voice crying 'Save'
And recognised its meaning
For we knew so much of repentance and of sorrow,
Anger and sorrow for anger.
We say 'make love' as if we thought that we fashioned
The movements, emotions, wishes, longings and hopes
And O we were open to so much sadness. I asked you
'Can it be worth it? Will this last?' You answered
Simply by taking my hand and smiling and saying,

'Listen, the breeze is lifting the laden branches,
The thrush is making his annual music afresh
And the breeze is the bold conductor. Have no fear
Of love which costs so dear.'

I suppose I did not understand you and yet
I had known the fulfilment of trust, the first confidence
Of love, and also the awe which love induces.
So I took your hand and stared in your eyes and whispered
'There was pain once and I was frightened but now
You teach me the pain is needed, as in Spring
Birth breaks the egg, clouds spill in rain and there
Is hunger for Easter and doing penance. I'm learning
That love is only and deeply itself when repentance
Issues out to the world which needs to be saved.
My heart is saved by you, my mind is thronged
By old discarded wishes but softly among them
A music of Spring is sounding, is rising.' We walk
Into and through and out of the wood and pause
Not for words and only uncertainly for music.
I think we are waiting for Spring to return our childhood
And for childlike confession and hope. It is hope we have lost
But love is singing, is so excited and we
Are only a little part of a greater plan
Enacted at Easter over and over again
When we stretch our bodies under the noonday sun
And worship a God who is pain.

This is the meaning for all the coldness, the fraught
Mood, the angry arguments – but then
These do not last, love as surrender endures
And sings and dances under the blossom and sunlight.
A hand of forgiving light is laid on our heads
And love does not fear for the night.

All this is partly a prayer a child once heard
And partly invented when Spring brought the good tide in,
Tide of stream and river, the white wash of blossom,
And the child understands without speaking the song of the
    thrush
And the pulsing nerve of the lark.

Here is Spring and Lent and here is happiness
Even though three crosses stand and wait for death,
One death especially, love has taught us it is
Our only salvation. Love needs a death and a death
Is a man and a God moving and dying in springtime
But waking up and rising as stems push through earth.
A stone is moved, a rising is in the air
A human form is stepping along the grass.
It is walking as love always does, bearing a gift
And we take it as we have always accepted forgiveness,
Saying little but watching the bold sun lift
As the Easter footsteps pass.

An Easter Sequence

I *The Start of Holy Week*

How to be sad when the tulips swell in the wind,
When the hyacinth admires its own voluptuous smell,
When tit and sparrow, thrush and blackbird spend
Time out of mind building or singing well?
Yet this could have been the end.

The start of Holy Week was always full
Of quick excitement; enchantment, shouting, palms thrown down
Before a King who knew and tried to tell
That darkness comes, that suffering will crown
The hopes that meant so well.

I cannot make my mind dark but I can
Think of a death. I choose to force it back.
The shock, the dreadful pain, a pale-faced man
Who could or would not tell his sudden lack.
'It's all part of a plan'

Somebody said at the time and now once more
I can see the tulips glow, hear blackbirds sing
But know that life is mostly inner war
Until next Saturday when the stones will ring
On this beleaguered star.

II *Holy Week*

Time of water everywhere. The Spring
Sprinkles the land. There has been too long a drought.
Good drenchings come and brighten everything.
Time of water into wine and doubt
Flowering to faith. Birds sing

Matins and Lauds, O every hour indeed,
Bells ring, the spirit climbs beyond the sky
And touches a true Heaven. We have need
Of Eden, Paradise. All prayers fly
And we confess our greed,

Our lust and pride and anger, once again
Renew our trust, make promises we hope
To keep. O there is gladness in the rain,
We think of sorrow far beyond our scope
As Christ's wounds flower with pain.

He'll blossom on the cross in three weeks now,
The saviour of the world will die again.
He is the flower upon a hurting bough,
The crown of thorns and nails will give him pain
But the worst one is how

We go on daily wounding him and he,
Although he's out of time, still feels the great
Dark of betrayal. He's nailed on a tree
Each time we fail him. Suffering won't abate
Until the liberty

This God-Man gave us is used only for
Kindness and gentleness. Our world is full
Of dying Christs – the starved, the sick, the poor.
God sleeps in cardboard boxes, has no meal.
We are his torturer

Each time we fail in generosity,
Abuse a child or will not give our love.
Christ lets us use our fatal liberty
Against himself. But now and then one move
Of selflessness sets free

The whole of mankind whom he saw at play
And work as he hung dying, when his side
Was pierced. That spear was how we fail to say
We love someone, but each time tears are dried
It's Resurrection Day.

IV *Holy Saturday*

The open doors, statues are covered but
Soon there'll be flowers, a special candle and
Easter upon us. Daffodils are cut
And hyacinths blow perfume through the land,
But now we brood on what

The spirit freed from flesh can really mean
And how a resurrection happened. Death
Is emptiness, a vacuum. We have seen
Thousands of soldiers die this year, their breath
Stopped suddenly. Again

Violence, a short and distant war,
Conflict where Christ hung not long ago
Only but now and with us all and where
Our soldiers barely men were forced to show
A smile and not the fear

Which moved them most. Now Holy Saturday
Is the sweet smell of Spring. The land is rich
For celebration. Children dance and play.
Our thoughts of death will soon be out of reach
And all sin washed away.

V *Crucifixion*

Always the same and always new. The nails
Are hammered hard in every place we know
Upon our maps. Within all our bad wills
Our better choices echo. It seems so
Easy to see what fails

As someone else's fault, our parents' or
Some illness that we cannot prove was not
Responsible for deeds that we abhor.
And yet we have refreshing spells of doubt
And hate the subtle war

We wage within ourselves. We must look out
And Easter begs us to. It's blithe with Spring
When once again God's human body's put
Upon a cross to bear our suffering.
A little love can yet

Guide us to the place where other men
Copy the God of saving and take on
The unjust agony. Christ's holy pain
Is borne by his best children. Yes, the Son
Of God brings Easter in

When blossom covers thorn, when sweet fresh air,
Smelling of buds and leaves, compels us to
Honour this world that's not beyond repair.
Compassion is the only way to grow
And Christ is buried there.

VI *Easter*

Doubt has been so near all through this Lent
And also disbelief.
There has been war and its cold partner, death,
There has been argument.
War is close always now we move so fast,
And few are innocent

Except our children and also except
Nature run riot. Spring
Arrived so suddenly we were amazed
At its impulsive fling.
Resurrection is the mood and theme
And trust returns to sing.

But death still vexes. Many think it is
The absolute, cold end.
Yet even atheists feel hope and trust
And almost understand
Creation, order, purpose manifest.
Lord of victory, mend

The war-rent buildings and the broken minds,
The heart which cannot bear
More pain until it knows a God brought low
And almost to despair.
Quicken us, let us blossom and believe,
Risings are everywhere.

VII *Easter Morning*

(Mary Magdalen)

It was a good day with its panache when
This mourning woman walked into the garden.
She and two other women stayed when men –
Save John, his favourite – watched Christ leave his burden
Of flesh. She carried pain,

This Magdalen, but kept a little hope
And that is why she visited the tomb.
She could not know of life beyond our scope
Would raise him up. There was no longer room
Or time for him to sleep

And so he'd gone, but Magdalen could see
A radiant figure come and recognise
Her Lord and great forgiver. But when she
Came near he told her not to touch him. Eyes
Told her enough, set free

All grief and disappointment, so she went
To John and Simon Peter and they ran
A race toward that tomb. This huge event
Lit Nature up and showed how it began
And how all death was spent.

And so it is each year when Spring's about.
The Cross that flowered with pain must show a death,
A saving one to take away our doubt.
At Easter each breeze is a sweetened breath
When Christ comes walking out.

VIII *The Ascension*

Ascend and disappear but in what way?
How did this special man take on the clouds?
If he was God then God himself could play
With solar systems, see the frightened crowds
Look up, beg him to stay.

It is a mystery, and my creed declares
God made the planets, space and you and me,
Then every obstacle yields thoroughfares.
The chosen watched until they could not see
Him any more. Affairs

Against all reason, mysteries, miracles
Happen when we believe. Again last week
Christ took the clouds once more. My credo tells
Me this is so. Not mind but huge heartbreak
Has wrapped God-man away.

For Restraint

When will it come again
   An age when delight
Does not need to snatch or attain
   Possession at sight?
We have waited long enough
   For an age when love

Is not toyed with or only seen
   As something to own
And use. We have surely been
   Searching for pleasure alone,
Seen it as its own end.
   Let us understand

What we are searching for
   And when and why.
We are men who need to adore
   For whom one sigh
Can begin a near-perfect world.
   Love, it is called.

A Childhood Horror

I have pretended long, in loyalty.
I had a childhood hurt for five harsh years,
I let it wound my good fragility
And over decades I've shed many tears
And sometimes wished that I were wholly free
Of faith because it was to me all fears,

Unhappiness and, yes, grief for a part
That should be left untouched in childhood till
There have been many blows upon the heart.
I listened to the words within that still
Confessional. 'You must not be a part
Of the communion tomorrow.' Frail

I was and still a child although fifteen.
My only fault was large uncertainty
Of my faith's tenets. I had not yet been
Close to grave sin. A dark shade stood between
Me and the altar. Gone was liberty
Yet absolution had just set me free.

The priest was twisted, sick. I felt no hate
For children think they cannot change such things
Or run from them. Of course it was too late
When later I could tell all this. Love sings
Now in my spirit but when black moods wait
For me I cannot launch them on light wings.

God, you meant terror once. But maybe this
Brought me close to your mysteries. I knew of
Unjust suffering. Deciding this
I sometimes now am filled with boundless love
And gratitude from which I've power to build
Music, the poem and all they are witness of.

Beyond the Horoscope

What does it mean, this spirit? What do we owe
To father, mother, all our forebears? Are
Our bodies which can agitate us so

Shaped back much further than we see, so far
That genes are mixed in such strange ways that we
Quite understandably say that a star

Or a whole galaxy has helped us be
This person now and that one then. We add
The readings up till we begin to see,

Or think we do, how curiously we're made.
Our blood and bone and free-will seem to move
To purposes beyond our choice. We fade

And dwindle into death yet know dreams of
Sweet everlastings, dignities so bold
That we believe beyond our being old.

For Louise and Timothy

Two years between them. Now Louise is ten
Or almost that. When there is trouble they
Unite at once and run and hide away.
Is this mere chance or else a chosen state
When a dark shadow mars a happy day?

I've thought this over and I've come to this –
Gentle Nature makes these allies when
Trouble's about. Often they're enemies,
My great-neice and great-nephew, yet it is
A kindly instinct when they guard the pain

Of one another or of both. They are
So swift in their alliance that I feel
An almost tearful gratitude where fear
Joins them together. This is like a war
Which has its moments when one heart can heal
Another's dread upon this stricken star.

Romantic Love

I thrive on incompletion and, in love,
Demand a distance which I cannot reach.
I inch up to it and it's on the move,
I feel so poor yet know that it is rich,
It's always moving off.

I've whispered sometimes and heard it reply,
I've stalked it and it seemed to stay quite still,
I've made a clumsy speech when I should sigh,
I've learnt this is an honest way to feel.
O may it never die.

For it is only thus that love stays new,
Starlike and with no touch of mine to make
The tender enterprise remain its true
Untarnished self. My heart indeed may break
But not such love also.

The Word

Think how it's teased and troubled, made a part
Of speech. The word is wonderful and trim
And speaks for thought or else a broken heart,
Is sweet and soft to her while it galls him.

None is pleased always, yet in poetry
When lucent language enters perfect mind
And music is the gist of harmony,
The word is absolute, both strict and kind.

And, at such pondering, I think of how
Saint John spoke of the 'Word', how it began
And stayed and reined the present. Priests will bow

And say 'This is' and God is given to man
Who eats the Bread and prays within a Now
That's gone too soon and God knows why and when.

Meditation

What is this I and what are you? I say
In utmost faith that we can truly meet
And know each other, not on every day
And not on every path or in each street
    But as a blessing now and here.
      We fashion what we are

By will and by all things we love and those
Exempla, active models, soul and breath,
Losers of self, in part what others chose
To make of us before the brink of death.
    We feel indeed that we shall last
      And outstrip present, past

And make a moving future which the clock,
The plane, the ship, the car know nothing of.
However much we may pretend or mock
We are so sure that there's no end of love.
    Death is an edge where we must stand
      And not, hope tells, an end.

We tatter, fray, our patchwork's seldom whole
But, now and then, we are surprised into
The master of our own intrinsic soul
Which leads us where we've never learnt to know,
    Yet we can recognise the state
      Where our death has no date.

An Age of Doubt

They stay there on an impulse
A seed, a star, an explosion
And all creation followed on this, and design
Was really haphazard. I never shall believe it.
I stare tonight at a late-March sky and see stars
Distributed in patterns we have found
And named and taken over.
Atheists say with certainty all this started
By chance, that there's no maker.

Once, after a childhood full of trust
And hope and faith, I suddenly felt unsure,
Thought of the Holy Ghost as a huge bird
Which I knew did not exist.
After that, doubt followed doubt, nothing was certain,
I wanted my faith and trust back, longed for the sure
Days of childhood. They would not return.
For months, no, years, I lived in doubt. I read
Books of philosophy, they gave further doubts,
Ones I had never heard of.
This was the doubt of life, my late adolescence,
I thought that growing up meant loss of innocence,
Hated my altering body.
My mind, so wide once with imagined kingdoms,
Shrivelled and shrank to doubt of my own existence,
Let alone of God's or of another's.
My dear, delightful days of saying Mass,
Of moving in dreams of angels all about me
Disappeared and I was alone, one doubt
And not even sure of that.

Gradually, O so slowly and discreetly
Faith crept back, stars reappeared in patterns.
And what brought this about?
I was reading poems, falling in love with verse,
With Keats and his nightingale and Grecian urn,
With Coleridge and his Ancient Mariner,
Wordsworth near Tintern Abbey.
And soon I started to write my small attempts

At the art of verse. I entered a huge family,
A place where poetry sang and was applauded,
Where love was how a stanza whispered its way
Above a starlit forest,
And my rhythms tried to copy the tides' huge impulse,
Dover Beach, most of all.
And, unlike Matthew Arnold's, my waves came in
With ships of certainty putting their anchors down
And settling in the jetties of *my* country,
And I gazed at the full and half and quarter-moon
And the stars all seemed to surrender to obvious music
Conjured by poets making a potent song.
So I began to feel a little, O such a little
But so authentic a power, it altered my poems
Whose rhythms sometimes moved to the tide of creation
And felt the touch of a God.

First Love

I only felt it when somebody said
   'She likes you. Did you know?'
I did not and now thoughts ran through my head.
   My heart was touched also,
O but with so much tenderness and so
Much hope. About me all the new Spring spread

And moved in breezes I could understand
   But never could explain.
I did not even want to hold her hand
   And this love gave no pain,
Not even that kind sort we can't defend.
Here was first love. The world was new again.

Such sweetness lasted long and time had yet
   No power. I learnt of care
And joyous admiration, welcomed it.
   I did not need to share
Or speak of this. I had no wish to set
Words down about it. Love was everywhere.

How long this lasted I shall never know.
   Time and memory came
Together in an absolute sweet now.
   Enough to hear her name
And watch from far-off. On the Eden bough
The apple hung again. Love held no shame.

Today I shed tears longing to learn how.

For the Young

What have we done? What have we made for you?
A world of violence lies all around,
And you are now part of the violence too.
You can't do anything without the sound

Of beating drums and screaming yells. You are
Not used to silence but have grown up with
Natural discord, inner and outer fear,
Dark sky above you, loud noise underneath.

It is our fault but we have lost the right
To discipline you to a gentle world.
Often your love-making's a tender sight.

You cling as if you almost had to hold
The world in place. You throw a gracious light
And show quiet ways in which you can be bold.

The Start of the Universe: April 1992

They've heard the echoes of the starting stars,
They say, these physicists. I am amazed
And feel the sky is shrinking. Is it Mars
Or Saturn signalling? So they have blazed

A trail for us and some conclude this means
Chance is the master and creation is
A random happeninng. Yet each star leans
Upon our reckoning, and the galaxies

Shrink to our telescopes. I never thought
Creation could be easy or took place
In seven actual days. Now I am caught

Up with the physicists' conclusions, trace
Mankind's beginning to a wonder wrought
Aeons of echoes back, each one a grace.

Inner and Outer

It was always a danger to me, this inward-turning
Search between doubt and doubt, search for a truth.
In childhood, I think, came the first warning
When I told lies as stories. In my youth

Self caught me up and made me my own doubt,
My eyes turned in and were amazed to see
A kind of kingdom turned all inside-out.
It baffled me. I wanted certainty.

Now I look out, so many decades later
And cannot have enough of what I see
Up there, beyond beyond. I see a better

Proof of purpose in each galaxy.
Now every poem is a kind of letter
Posted to stars yet somehow sent by me.

Curtains Undrawn

Looking in windows down a night-time street
    In Winter, I don't feel
A *voyeur*, no, I only seem to meet
    Lives lived with love's good will.

There is a student with an angle-poise
    Lamp. He's hard at work
In happy concentration. There's no noise
    As yet and nothing's stark

Or ugly. I've a sense of neighbourhood,
    Of being near yet keeping
A proper distance. Now I find it good
    To think of children sleeping

With night-lights on. No doubt their parents will
    Later go up to bed
And make love without speaking. There's a still
    Design within my head

As if I were about to write a score
    To fit these modest lives
Where there are quarrels sometimes but no more
    Than small ones which arrive

Because we are imperfect. I walk on
    Under a full moon's stare,
Knowing that elsewhere crimes are done –
    Not here, no, never here,

And 'here' is much more usual, I believe,
    Than war and hate and dread
Since here are still lives where the trust of love
    Will never be quite dead.

Say I am sentimental. I don't care.
  The rooted tree of trust
I know is always flowering somewhere
  Where people still are just.

Maybe they could not tell you what they think
  Their lives are all about.
Philosophies grow cold, most dogmas shrink
  Here where hope's not in doubt.

Time in Summer

Summer bedevils the clocks. They tick away
Into themselves. As heat grows stronger we
   Forget them, do not need them, breathe within
Another element. We are all space
   And easy air while the good time of day

Sounds from the stable clock or city chime.
The heat hangs on, a shimmering garment in
   The drumming air. We are but half-awake
And half-a-dreaming. We are moods of warmth,
   Our tepid foreheads are not damp with time

But with the season's moisture. Fountains play
Temptingly far away. A tiny stream
   Is loud with falling water. All's a haze
And we are mere suggestions, half-ideas
   That somebody may soon begin to say.

First Confession

So long ago and yet it taunts me still,
That First Confession. I was only seven
When I first knelt by that impersonal grille
And poured my little sins out one by one.
I never felt near God or any Heaven.
It was my thefts which made all that undone

Or never started. Certainly the priest
Was not unkind though he told me I must
Return those things. I think my childhood ceased
Upon that day. My spirit had been light
And happy for six years. I lost my trust
And learnt a little of the spirit's night.

From that day on this healing sacrament
Was hurting for me. No-one's fault, it's true,
And yet I think the child's right element
Of joy should not be risked so early but
Left till youth sends doubt and darkness through
Flesh and soul and childhood's door slams shut.

Green

Green.
Green for our fear of what we have spoilt, from the
                                                    turning
Wave to the grass that rots as we look, the roots
    Which break in the ground. What green-sickness
                                                 there is
In the world we walk on; look up, too, from the edge
    Of a field to the centre of cities where pollution
Stands in the air, blows to the suburbs, then
    Runs through corn and fruit-trees, renders barren
The bushes of blackberries, fields of strawberries, all
    That we ate with relish, bottled once and set
On a high and treasured shelf. We have set ourselves
    Too high too often, thought we ruled the sky,
Owned the arable farmlands, had a say
    In sunlight, starlight, all that atmosphere
Was rich in once. Not any longer. We have
    Watched the foxes run and die, have seen
Pigeon and pheasant fall from the sky to our feet,
    And felt exultant. Almost too late we learn
Our lesson. We need a purity, a cleansing
    Ritual for the actual. We must unlearn now,
But all too slowly or else too hectically fast,
    That we must honour the earth and the flying birds,
Not spray chemicals on the delicate buds
    And poison the later fruit. We have been greedy
With land and air but also lecherous;
    We sow our seed too widely and in wrong places
So that we hinder a baby's growth, produce
    A handicapped race. We must be sorry and make
A fertile penitence, look about us, let
    Nature teach us once again. O can
We walk the difficult steps back to Eden garden
    And place the apple back on the poisoned tree?
Is it too late? Not if we deepen our sorrow,
    Give where we used to take, feed orphans, snatch
A million Christ-children back from the three-fold world
    Where the Holy Trinity broods with a lucky number.
So in a green dream of sweet fertility let us

Kneel in sorrow, carefully plant our seeds
And exhale good air and leave it to others too,
    May the green, unpolluted waves turn over and over
Till green is the colour of safety and survival,
    And may green be our freshness for the last redemption.

Think Of

Think of a note
And a drop of water
Falls and splashes and
See the taut blue
And a cloud cruising, a
Golden shaft of
Riches and
Then comes a theme,
An easy drift,
A pluck on a harp, a
Call on a horn
And then see
In the mind's eye
In the heart's ear
In the reaching hand
And the beat of a heart
To a somewhere coming
Choir of angels
Where seraphs blow
A trumpet of sound
And a colour enters
Imagination's
Ajar door
And we are aware
Of a threshold crossed
Of a shadow woven
In webs of air
And more of all
Always more and more

Spell for a Dead Baby

You filled a gentle pause in air
    But would not stay for long,
And yet you've left a magic here
    Still delicate yet strong
Enough for us to think of waste.
    We've racked our brains to find
A spell of words that suits you best.
    They will not come to mind.
Then let this wish of ours at least
    Serve to remind, remind.

Cold Words

I learn of love now that I've been betrayed
In such a little way. Friendship was more
Important than I knew. No words were said

But only wrong ones written. Why were there
No thanks, no greetings? When I am alone
Childhood is back and its hot tears are here

Burning my cheeks at midnight. I have known
Love-affairs broken as all of those who care
Have learnt. But I feel coldness to the bone

Because possessiveness had played no part
In this good friendship I'd known for five years.
Now I have lost what seemed a grace of heart,

A reciprocity and I shed tears
Because there is no reason for such cold
Shunning. I spoke little of my fears,

But much of my friend's life, I was not bold
And did not make demands. Why have I lost
What seemed so shared and kind? Let me be fooled,

Not cynical but still keep my whole trust,
That childhood gift I've carried from the past.

Ordination

for Richard Finn O.P.

Hats fit for a wedding. Here and there
A crawling child, a cry. There is a crowd
Rustling and waiting. They are gathered here
For an occasion that is kind and proud,
The centre of your life, another start.
Some are near tears and in my waiting heart

There is a stirring as, perhaps, I knew
When I first saw the sea or when I met
Someone important to my life. For you
There's love and preparation, no regret.
You smile, seem calm. Your friends are all around
But there's no silence. Every little sound

Promises what your future means. You'll pour
Water on babies' heads and speak their name.
You walk with Christ and you have known him for
Most of your life but now it's not the same.
You make hard vows, are taken up by grace
Which somehow spreads to all in this good place.

But there's also the largest gift of all
That you receive. You'll take the wine and bread
And speak right words and Christ himself will fill
These simple things. He rises from the dead,
He lets you touch his side but with rich faith,
Still wine and bread but all God underneath.

I've known you only for four years and yet
You asked me here. I see you smile. We take
Your blessing. All your free-will now will set
You on a course where there will be heart-break
And maybe doubt, though not for long. I wish
You peace and thanks as you give me God's flesh.

Star-Gazing

Give it a name. It is still there,
One on its own, another star
  Which is not yours and is not mine.

And yet we need to find a name,
To lay indeed a kind of claim,
  A beauty wrought to our design.

But we are wrong. We don't possess
The stars. Our words make them grow less
  As we waylay them to define.

They shine a love. Another one
Is there tonight. The Summer sun
  Left the horizon's steady line.

Think, there are more than we can count,
Star after star, O such amount,
  Each seems to flicker out a sign,

To hand a message. It is this:
'We are much further than you guess
  And brighter too. Yes, we combine

Distance and light to give a show
Like fireworks which retain their glow,
  We keep a rich unmeasured shine.'

The voices pause. I look again,
The sky is pouring silver rain
  Which could be yours and might be mine.

Light Between Leaves

The light between the leaves and under the leaves –
        Do not forget these,
The mouth which turns and touches, the eye which loves,
        Here are our ecstasies

Or some of them. They started long ago
        Back in our infancies,
Others came later when there was pain to know
        But there are always those

Treasures of kindness, comfort during grief,
        Learnt opportunities,
But now the Summer leaves are full of life
        And teach us mysteries.

Nothing is usual, nothing commonplace,
        Nothing easy to please,
There is a sky of comets in a loved face,
        A thousand astronomies.

The leaves are turning under an easy wind,
        The evening starts to cool
And love moves gently in a shared state of mind
        And comforts and makes us whole.

A Question of Form

The point is that a Monet does not move,
A Mozart clarinet sonata can't
Be seen or smelt. Art works by metaphor
And cool constriction. Cool means white-hot here.
By rule and lack of liberty art's meant

To work and at its best it does so. Last
Tuesday I was heckled by a boy
Who said that poetry never should be cast
In form, but come without control and fast.
I knew that all this had to do with joy

And pleasure. Why did I not think to say
Nature has limitations? Trees can't move
Away from roots. They only grow that way.
I said 'Form's not a jelly-mould to pour
A poem inito. It can only say
Whatever is its message.' But I saw

That none of this convinced, yet Baudelaire
Juggled the senses. Language smelt and could
Taste, but still switched senses had to say
Their mood and tone in form. All art can play
But always is contained, leashed in. The good
Work of art makes laws it must obey.

Song

A violin waits for its sound,
  A poem for its word.
Listen, up from the ground
  Rises the lyric bird.

It possesses no instrument
  Save its own taut throat
But it offers us eloquence
  In a single note.

Remember the blackbird who
  Could not cease to sing,
The power of its voice grew
  Beyond Summer and Spring,

Beyond Winter and Fall.
  The dumb violin
Is unused but the blackbird's call
  Makes our world begin.

Death

How do we think and feel and sense? What happens
  When we come to our death?
Is there a darkness or a purpose that opens
  When we reach our last breath?
My creed insists that all that is good in us opens
  And finds itself held with

A magnitude of thought, a wonder, a kind
  Of world where we perfect
What went astray, what faltered and kept the mind
  Tormented, unhappy and racked
On its own bad past. And so we are refined
  And ready to connect

Spirit with spirit, but I cannot conceive
  Of a state where every sense
Is no longer needed. It is hard to believe
  In such a circumstance,
And yet my creed exhorts me to behave
  In this world for the chance

Of living with its Creator. I'm thinking of
  A time when I was ten
And went out in the dark, saw stars above
  And felt drawn out of then
And there. I was upheld by a new love
  And I do not know when

I was drawn out of that uplifted state
  But when at last I was,
Even in childhood ignorance, I knew what
  Is meant by gift and grace,
And now I think that death may be like that
  Undeserved blessedness.

For under those stars my senses were set aside,
   I saw further than sight,
I knew an order then that would not divide
   My spirit from that night.
Within its lofty presence I could hide
   In joy outsoaring delight.

In the Beginning

In the beginning, on the first true dawn
Our lives began. No clocks or watches were
There to intrude. An aeon made a song,

Ten million years went by and even more
Until the angel came upon a breeze,
Bearing a message and the girl was there

Absorbed by calm, using free-will which is
The nub of our salvation. God was young
And slipped into our time, but all of this

Rested on her. The child was small among
All angry drifts but Mary kept her word
And it grew in her womb, was nine months long

Like us but not like us. There was no room
For him from the beginning. God could trust
Himself to our caprice, would know the tomb

And save us from the misrule of our dust.

In Praise of Giotto

Giotto, lover of tenderness, you were
The first great painter who showed man as man,
Not icon or pure spirit but entire,
For through the flesh the best compassion ran.

You taught this when you painted Joachim
And Anna, Mary's parents, standing with
Their faces close and intimate. In him
Was gratitude, in her, surrender. Death

You also knew was glad surrendering
Without a dread. So God himself was laid
Gently in his tomb, all suffering

Wiped from his face. You understood men prayed
And found right peace when they could speak and sing
As Francis did for whom the birds delayed.

For the Times

I must go back to the start and to the source,
Risk and relish, trust my language too,
For there are messages which need strong powers.
I tell their tale but rhythm rings them true.

This is a risky age, a troubled time.
Angry language will not help. I seek
Intensity of music in each rhyme,
Each rhythm. Don't you hear the world's heart break?

You must, then, listen, meditate before
You act. Injustices increase each day
And always they are leading to a war

And it is ours however far away.
Language must leap to love and carry fear
And when most grave yet show us how to play.

The Way They Live Now

You make love and you live together now
Where we were shy and made love by degrees.
By kiss and invitation we learnt how
Our love was growing. You know few of these

Tokens and little gifts, the gaze of eye
To eye, the hand shared with another hand.
You know of few frustrations, seldom cry
With passion's stress, yet do you understand

The little gestures that would mean so much,
The surging hope to be asked to a dance?
You take the whole of love. We lived by touch

And doubt and by the purposes of chance
And yet I think our slow ways carried much
That you have missed – the guess, the wish, the glance.

The Poem in Itself

The poise of time. The history of speech.
Articulation. Subject brought to heel.
The poem is filled and animated, rich
With hints and hopes, with how you wish to feel.

It won't be faked or ever forced. You must
Seek out its landscape even when it's yours.
The attitude for you is total trust
Not of your own but of the poem's powers.

It is a gift, a spell, a fabric wrought
Seamless. It also is a way to pray
By which I mean it's ceremonious thought

Spoken through you. You must not let it stray.
It asks for silence sometimes, won't be bought.
It's given, yet commands you to obey.

Parents

You are two, you are seven, you are ten
And never more than fifteen years or so,
You are always seen as you were then.
Parents never notice what you grow

Into in your twenties, thirties, more.
They lose the sense of time, ignore the watch
And chiming clocks. When you have lost the score
Of teens and twenties, they will never catch

Up with you. It is your task to keep
A bold pretence up, be the age they want
To see you as, be kind, forget the leap

Of time you made when you left home. Repent
Of ancient tempers lost. Within their minds
You have not changed but still are innocent.

Innocence

I almost loved you but in friendship's kind
And unpossessive way. Now something's gone
Wrong. An expert darkness fills my mind
But I can find no reason why my sun

Of gracious feeling has been shadowed with
Such unexpected night. Friendship has run
Into cover and a little death
Mocks at the very rigour of the sun.

Shall I write and ask what has gone wrong?
No, I feel it may bring some new hurt.
I speak low words when once I would have sung

For the pure issue of my ready heart.
All I can hope is silence won't last long
But waiting has become a new, flawed art.

Two Sonnets of Art and Age

I

Let there be orchestras for my last words
Or, better yet, no words but only sound
Diminishing, increasing like the birds
Rising and climbing from the dewy ground

Of dawn. I would hear melody and know
Someone, much luckier, may find words to fit.
Dying I would hear only the undertow
Of purest sound and the rich tone of it.

Names are for all the living and the young.
Young poets shall find words I never seek,
I knew another purpose for my song –

It told the story of how hearts will break.
The young are proud and agile with their throng
Of bold sensation praised for its own sake.

II

Let there be quiet, almost only still
Moments when I stop writing and begin
To know that pages wait for me to fill
Them with glad battles I was proud to win.

Battle with form and style, with metaphor,
Power over rhyme, an art grown very near
To prized perfection. While I wrote the score
I found I only learnt how I could fear

The noise of time, life's hurry, love's regret.
I filled up many pages with these things
And sometimes language seemed to take on wings.

Perfection was an end I never met
But O I loved the way that poetry sings
And feels most strong when sun begins to set.

Two Sonnets for a Czech Friend

for R.

I

Long ago she was a refugee,
My Czech friend whom I've never seen in rage.
We met in hospital. It seemed to me
She was not ill but quiet. Her own true age

Meant nothing for her courtesy was more
Like a good child's than someone grown-up, yet
Her discipline was wise and adult for
She suffered very quietly. I've met

Many with breakdowns or depression but
None like her who felt her country's pain
By hearing voices, sometimes throwing out

Her treasures like a tribute. Was she not
Living her country's anguish once again
Who never once complained about her lot?

II

It seemed most suitable that my Czech friend's
Country should know a bloodless revolution.
She was invited to relearn her land's
Sights. She brushed her Czech up like a lesson

And seemed excited, eager to depart.
But when the time to go was near she would
Not eat or drink and on the day to start
She could not speak. It was because she's good

That my friend could not go back to her land.
It was not fear that stopped her but a mind
At one with all its pain. I understand

This now in hindsight. Still my friend repined
For all those deaths as if to lend a hand
By dying slowly with her own lost kind.

88

Poetry Sometimes...

Sometimes you have to lead it by the hand
As if it were a child which you must teach.
Sometimes you write what you don't understand
Or only partly. Words climb out of reach

But for that reason, need not be set by.
The more I write, the less I seem to know
What this strange business is, since poetry
Like this, like that can come about or go

Beyond imagining. I only know
That it's not at my beck and should not be.
It takes me late or early, makes me grow

Up overnight. It is a way to see,
To learn, to celebrate. It's given too,
And uses me yet offers liberty.

November Sonnet

Spirit of place. Spirit of time. Re-form
The rugged oaks and chestnuts. Now they stand
Naked and pallid giants out of storm
And out of sorts. It is the Autumn's end

And this is Winter brought in by All Saints
Fast followed by All Souls to keep us in
Touch with chill and death. Each re-acquaints
Us with the year's end. Yet we now begin

A life of realism, watching out
For a red sunset, grateful for a dawn
Of rich light now. Tall shadows step and strut

Facing the big wind daily coming on
Faster. This is the season of right doubt
While that elected child waits to be born.

Water and Air

The eddy is a coil, a sliver, then
Gone to become a waterfall far off,
Perhaps a total brimming with its spume
When staring once can never be enough.

How time and space are one when water is
The drift and flow, the topic, later still
An image of all elements, a trace
Of almost a free spirit which we feel

As thought is felt in concentration and,
When you look up, you feel a world of strain.
The argument you hoped to understand

Has eddied elsewhere to return as rain
Cooling a forehead like a sea-dipped hand.
Water and air draw near again, again.

Beyond

The pith, the nub, the nap, the rough, the feel
And grasp of things. I praise what pleases touch,
Heartens the eyes, trances nose to tell
What ear awaits. I close my eyes to reach

The essence under each thing but I can't
Go further than the overcoat, the pile
That covers things. My senses try to hurl
Beyond but are set by. I wait a while,

Hoping that patience may invite the tall
Spirit of sky. Its stars alone I reach
And they should be enough, but I yet call

Vainly perhaps, the power that bows to teach
Meanings. O never mind, love's made of all
That leans to touch and finds its perfect pitch.

In the Nursery

We had no need of toys. Domestic things
Were transformed into objects used at Mass:
For thurible a tin train on thick strings,
A toy stove was a tabernacle. These

Were sacred in our game which always was
A serious one. We mumbled gibberish
Instead of Latin. So a holy place
Was once a nursery. A childhood wish

Enacts the strict demands of art. Also
It shows how far man's rituals reach. We were
Priest and server. From such small things grow

Religious awe and love of art. With care
We copied what we'd seen as, to and fro
The censer swung and all was hallowed there.

Out of Time and Season

What is this joy? It is like love again
And yet there is no object. This is more
Than seeking or possessiveness. The rain
Pleases, the sky is blue, April is here

But long before its time. Daffodils throng
Wherever there is grass. Birds carol too.
There is an inspiration in their song,
There is a sweetness now that passes through

My nerves and blood. But it drives further yet,
My spirit is engaged and I can feel
A power that is not mine search the sunset

And how I look at it. Upon me steal
Purposes out of time and so I let
Them have their way. They bless me and they heal.

Time and Love

It is all seasons and no time at ease,
The hour's evasive and the minute's in
A teasing mood. The sun is out to please
But later there's a moon which can begin

With its thin crescent, thoughts of love so soon
Waxing and then upon the wane again.
Today the sun is summer and at noon
It was unthought of to suggest that rain

Was needed for the land. But love has needs
And it will barter childhood friendships and
Then be so kind, we think its telling beads.

O love is careful not to understand
Until the cooling starts. It shapes its creeds
For you and me and time runs through our hands.

Subject and Object

It is most rife in Spring, this sudden move
From mind to object with no space between.
It comes as an immediate act of love
When what is wanted is what we have seen.

Maybe all looking is a love-affair
And it was the Impressionists who taught
Most accurately how the eyes can stir
The heart and all that in between is caught.

So on this mid-May morning when I drew
The curtains back, the first mist took me by
Imagination's storm, so fast I knew

Subject and object are both one, and I
Felt, saw this happen and I say it's true
And I don't need to ask the reason why.

Left in Charge

For Anne

No ghosts haunt here or, if they do, they are
Kindly and gentle. When I climb the stairs
There are no creaking steps. I see one star
Greeting me through a window which lays bare

A happy street. Young voices come and go.
A train moves in the distance and it brings
Back echoing times when childhood days went slow
And sleep came quickly. All about are things –

Books, paintings, statues – chosen with large care.
Nothing is unsafe for the children who
Come often to my host who is elsewhere.

Her love has left this house to me. I know
Trust and joy which fill the scented air
Took quiet days and nights to stay and grow.

Trees

We took them all for granted, these bold trees,
Wandered in the pools of dark they spread,
Lay down in afternoons when not a breeze
Blew the oaks' curls. Always overhead
Huge parasols protected and with these
Above we did not move until sun shed

Its long intolerably hot light and
Moved down the sky like silent troops at last
Released from drill. The broad kind chestnut's hand
Lay on us like a blessing. As trees cast
Their deeper shadows we saw sunlight send
Rich oils upon the canvas of the west.

Oak, ash and birch – each has a character
Shaped by long knowledge of the heat and cold.
These are contemplatives when no winds stir
Their ample branches. They are also bold
In their defiance of the sun. They share
The wisdom which belongs to all things old.

August Heat

There is a feeling of farewells today
  Although the August heat is all around.
There is no fountain anywhere to play,
  We need the water's sound.

The very word of it reminds of sea
  And river unpolluted. Children run
Into tubs of water nakedly.
  They feel the sun upon

Their flesh as gracious though they need no word.
  So very far back it has always been
Since we were happy with a clear thing heard
  Or good things only seen.

The mood of metaphysics takes us by
  A rough hand when we start to grow away
From this sweet sensuous world. The half-orb sky
  We think needs words we say,

As if all honest happiness were made
  By any expert way we think or feel.
It does its own wish, will not be obeyed
  By words. O words can kill

When watchful meditation is enough,
  Enough also the kindly fragrant air.
Why can't we be contented just to love
  As children do? We are

Unwise and often know it. Now today
  The feeling of farewells is sweet. It falls
When everything seems standing very still.
  Even the soft bird-calls

Move towards evening. Surely we are made
  For some place which endures beyond the hour.
We almost cry when day begins to fade,
  Loss has so great a power

O let things go. They must. We cannot make
      Anything stand or stay. Nothing is free.
We partly are but cunning love won't break
      And only love will be

Left when the sun has gone and breezes come
      And birds no longer try
To celebrate departures. Love's our home
      No matter how we try

To turn from it and plunder and lay waste.
      Even farewells must bow to it and go
Dwindling off. Even the mocking past
      Right love can overthrow.

Living by Love

It should be so and can be so I say.
We walk in love but keep dividing off
The play of hearts from what was only play:

Our childhood did not need to find a word
But lived it through. Grown-up we wish to lay
A claim on love. In childhood it was bared

And could teach hurt but mine did not. The way
My nurse would teach or mother kiss my hand
Was how a love was sealed, passion away

Elsewhere. I wish that it were thus today
But senses let loose passion and it's hard
To tame it. Love once did not need to say

That it ruled me and I was not afraid
Because I wished to stand a world away
And only worship from afar. I played

Love on a high but gentle note. Today
It is too harsh and deep, though love's a word
I try to live by and my poetry

Keeps me enclosed, well-ordered and close-barred.

An Old Story

They are all true, the images and rhymes
    That wish to speak of love.
Reason is magic, eternity is time's
    Master. We try to prove

A love like ours was never felt before
    Or never could excite
Others as it moves us. We've found a door
    That leads out of the night

To a perpetual day. That huge sunrise
    Is ours alone it seems
And so it is until that vowed love dies
    And lives in others' dreams.

When I Was Young

When I was young I wrote about the old.
Now I am old I write about the young.
The words are cautious for a worried world
And out of them I shape a tell-tale song.

I was irresponsible and wild
When I was young but now the young ones are
Thoughtful and anxious though their eyes are mild
Even when they speak to me of war.

They are prepared and do not blame the old
That many have to make the street their home.
I warm myself at their kind hearts. The cold
Shivers through me now long dark nights have come.

O but there is a joy that I would speak.
I have a dream and turn it to a song.
It is the only home that I can make.
Its doors are open to the careful young.

Movement and Meaning

Language is always on the move
　　Its meanings will not last for long
We try to call it back when love
　　Beckons us to shape a song.

But it's impatient, will not stay
　　Or be at any beck of ours
And yet it's we who help it play
　　And change the purpose of its powers.

It limits us for it's precise
　　And hates the superficial guise
Of novel meanings, has a nice
　　Neat purpose, will not generalise.

It flies higher than a kite
　　And dives more deep than submarines.
If we take care, its yoke is light
　　But if we falsely generalise

It moves away and closes like
　　The shiest mollusc in the sea
But when we are expert to strike
　　It opens to us instantly.

In ballad, dirge or lullaby
　　It moves to measures which we find.
It puts a meaning in a sigh
　　And heartbeats in a lucid mind.

Leavings

Going again and you
  Staring at me. The sky
Is a cruel blue.
  When will you and I

Get used to a probable trust,
  Be sure this is not the end?
Some love is always lost.
  Neither lover nor friend

Turns to look around
  After their seeing-off.
But when one has returned
  There is increase of love.

Witchery

I know witchery
Of words. I've seen them grow
High as the sun, or low
As trees' roots. Nature is
A kind of magic. We
Never get used to this
Power that's only hers.
She hides her purposes.

Sometimes in love or thought
I've felt my heart beat so
Fast I could not tell what
Had caused it, yet I know
It was a kind of spell.
Seers go direct
To what all thinkers must
Find with patient skill.
O, love, the world is tossed
To us. It will not spill.

A Father after his Daughter's Wedding

What was an instinct turns to vivid loss.
    The girl is married now,
His only daughter will not come across
    The threshold to endow
The home with joy and trouble weariness.
He would take all. A little happiness

Shaped at her birth and growing every year
    Seems precious now indeed.
He would disperse so often any fear
    Of any sort. His need
Is greater than the one invading her.
He is not jealous, no. He wants her life
Without him to be joyful, yet it's grief

Which he now feels. He has a little son
    And loves him but in ways
Quite different from the strong and urgent one
    He felt for her. His days
Are now a little empty but he will
Say nothing for he loves her mother still

In body and in spirit, and he draws
    Nearer to her. Their son
Is to them both often a careless cause
    Of worry. Life strides on
As love twines in and out in its quiet dance –
A gift, almost a fate, and yet not chance.

The Happy Regrets

Last words for my mother

Who knows how much I owe? So many things.
You had no rage but always could calm mine,
Were always ready with your comfortings
And also ready at pain's slightest sign
And as though with wings

You'd fly and fold me in your arms. When I
Was ill you once kept up a fire all night
And scarcely slept. At any childhood cry
You came with comfort. You had blue eyes bright
With wisdom. Now you lie

Under a small rose tree. It's April and
Your birthday has just passed. I thought of you
Last night and wished that you could understand
The gratitude I often could not show.
You were the one who'd mend

Misunderstandings. Sometimes people took
Your love for granted. I regret the days
When I was thoughtless, too lost in a book
To notice your compassion. Now your gaze
Comes to me when I look

At children being comforted, at old
People who have no words to tell their need.
You had the gift for finding seams of gold
In most unlikely purposes. You freed
My mind, made my heart bold.

You died in Winter eighteen months ago
And it was unexpected. I am glad
You never knew long pain. I want to show
How you taught guileless love and I am sad
Tonight I can't say so.